SPORTS ACADEMY

SPORTS STAR

IN TRAINING

SPORTS ACADEMY

STUDENT PASS

Name ....

First published 2019 by Kingfisher
an imprint of Macmillan Children's Books
The Smithson, 6 Briset Street, London EC1M 5NR
Associated companies throughout the world
www.panmacmillan.com

Series editor: Kath Jewitt
Design: Jeni Child

ISBN 978-0-7534-4483-2

9 8 7 6 5 4 3 2 1

1TR/0819/WKT/UG/128MA

A CIP catalogue record for this book is available from the British Library.

Printed in China

Picture credits
The Publisher would like to thank the following for permission to reproduce their material.
Top = t; Bottom = b; Centre = c; Left = l; Right = r
iStock: tomazl 24bl; Merlas 24br; sbayram 32–33; Michl 33t; vm 33c; Wildcow 32c; vm 33c; filrom: ViktoriiaNovokhatska 41bl Shutterstock: sportpoint 24bl, 24bc; Alex Bogatyrev 24br; Leonard Zhukovsky 25b; Oleksii Sidorov 26b; EFKS 26t; Adam Vilimek 27b; Krivosheev Vitaly 27t.

SPORTS STAR

IN TRAINING

KINGFISHER

Can you find the
cup on every page?

SPORTS ACADEMY

TRAINING PROGRAMME

BANG!

THEORY pages are full of important information that you need to know.

PRACTICAL pages have a task to do or a skill to acquire. Tick each page when you have completed that part of your training.

GOT WHAT IT TAKES?

So you want to be an athlete?
Are you brimming with energy and eager to learn?
Are you ready to work hard and train through the pain?
Then welcome to the Sports Academy!

HOW TO BE A TOP ATHLETE

Master these skills to be the best athlete you can be:

 1 **CONCENTRATION**
Train your brain
to only think about
what you are doing.

 3 **DETERMINATION**
Don't give up when
the going gets tough.
Try again and you
will improve.

 2 **CO-ORDINATION**
Make your arms,
legs and body parts
work together.

 4 **DEDICATION**
Put lots of time
into training to
really succeed.

PICK YOUR KIT

Choose four
items for your
kit bag.

a)

b)

c)

d)

e)

f)

g)

h)

SPORTS STAR INTERVIEWS

Match each sports star with their quote.

diver

road cyclist

pole vaulter

wheelchair racer

baseball player

A
"The races I compete in last for weeks and are thousands of kilometres long."

B
"I need strong arms to power around the track at 30 kilometres per hour."

C
"I wear a glove to help me catch the ball, which has been hit or thrown."

D
"I throw myself head-first off a board that is taller than a two-storey house."

E
"With the help of my pole, I can jump over a bar that's higher than a giraffe."

How many other types of sports stars can you think of?

TRAINING TIPS

◯ Keep training regularly and you will improve.

◯ Don't push yourself too hard or you might get injured.

◯ Set goals for yourself so you have something to aim for.

THEORY 2

SPORT FINDER

There are so many sports to choose from, but which one is right for you? Just answer the questions and follow the trails on this sport finder map.

START HERE

THEORY NO: 2

tick here

APPROVED

SPRINTING, HIGH JUMP or LONG JUMP

... could be for you

Are you good at catching, kicking or hitting a ball?

YES   NO

YES   NO

Are you a fast runner?

TENNIS, BADMINTON or TABLE TENNIS

... could be for you

NO

Do you like playing with others?

YES

NOT FOUND YOUR DREAM SPORT? THERE ARE PLENTY MORE TO DISCOVER. JUST READ THIS BOOK...

TRAMPOLINING, GYMNASTICS or FIGURE SKATING
... could be for you

YES

Are you bendy and good at balancing?

NO

NO

Are you brave and fighting fit?

YES

JUDO, TAEKWONDO or KARATE
... could be for you

SKIING, SKI JUMPING or SNOWBOARDING
... could be for you

YES   **NO**

Do you like getting wet?

NO

Are you fearless and ready for adventure?

YES

FOOTBALL, BASEBALL, BASKETBALL or CRICKET
... could be for you

SWIMMING, DIVING, CANOEING or ROWING
... could be for you

9

FOOD FOR FITNESS

It's your first day at the Academy and you need to fuel up ready for action. Grab a plate and tuck into some tasty food at the athletes' canteen.

Meat, fish, eggs, seeds, nuts and beans

TODAY'S MENU

 ○ **Carbohydrates** give you the energy you need for exercise.

 ○ **Proteins** help you grow and repair your body.

 ○ **Fats** give you a store of energy and keep you warm.

 ○ **Vitamins and minerals** keep your body healthy.

 ○ **Sugar and salt** should only be eaten in small amounts.

Potatoes, rice, pasta, noodles, cereals and breads

Fruit and veg are so healthy you need to gobble 5 portions a day!

Butter, milk, cheese, yogurt and dairy foods

Drink up! You need to glug down at least 8 glasses of water a day.

The colours show how much of each kind of food you should put on your plate.

Which foods will you pick to fill each section on the plate?

Protein

Fruit and veg

Carbohydrates

Dairy

11

"Ready? Do each exercise for 1 minute!"

1 March on the spot with high knees.

MUSCLES

When you exercise, your muscles call out for more energy and oxygen – the gas in the air we breathe.

You use an amazing 200 muscles just to take a single step!

PRACTICAL 2

WARM UP!

A good warm-up before training gets you ready for the hard work ahead! Look what happens inside your body when you get moving.

2 Circle your arms both ways.

SKIN

Exercise makes you warmer. Your body cools down by making a liquid called sweat, which comes out of tiny holes in your skin. As it dries it cools you.

PRACTICAL NO: 2
tick here
APPROVED

3 Jump from side to side.

4 Do star jumps.

BONES

When you walk, jump or run you put more weight on your bones and joints. Joints are the bendy places where bones meet.

○ elbow joint

○ knee joint

HEART

Your heart beats faster to pump more blood around your body. Your blood carries oxygen and energy from the food you eat to power your muscles.

○ heart

5 March and kick your heels back.

○ lungs

LUNGS

You breathe more quickly and take bigger breaths to suck in more oxygen.

SPORTING CHALLENGE

Your pulse rate is the number of times your heart beats in one minute.

1 Hold out one hand, palm up. Press two fingers onto your wrist below the thumb until you feel thumping.

2 Use a watch to count the thumps in one minute.

3 How many thumps do you count before exercise?

4 How many more do you count after some exercise?

TRAINING TIME

Could you work around the clock to get stronger, faster and fitter? Head for the training camp and find out what a normal day is like for a super swimmer.

7:00 am

○ Wake up and grab your training kit.

7:30 am

○ Eat healthy breakfast.

8:30 am

○ Hit the pool for swim training – 3 hours.

11:30 am

○ Eat a healthy lunch.

9:00 pm

○ Have a good night's sleep, ready for training tomorrow.

8:00 pm

○ Relax!

7:30 pm

○ Pack your kit ready for the next day's training.

6:30 pm

○ Eat a healthy dinner.

TRAIN YOUR BRAIN

Athletes imagine themselves scoring a perfect goal, or winning a race. Just thinking about an action helps your brain to control your body better.

12:30 pm

○ Relax and take a nap.

2:00 pm

○ Have a healthy snack before next training.

TV TIME

Athletes watch videos of themselves competing to see what they did right or wrong. They pick up tips by watching other top athletes in action too.

5:00 pm

○ Cool down with yoga and stretching.

3:00 pm

○ Work out at the gym to build strong arms and legs – 2 hours.

ACTIVITY

Spot five things that are wrong with the video clip above.

TRACK AND FIELD

Try out some sports at the track and field arena. Everywhere you look athletes are running, jumping or throwing things. Look out!

Athletes with disabilities use racing wheelchairs or special springy legs made from carbon to compete in track events.

Take a run up and jump into a soft sandpit. Some long jumpers can leap over 8 metres – that's as long as four beds put end to end!

Try to jump over a bar without knocking it off its posts. After each good jump, the bar is raised higher.

SPORTING CHALLENGE

- Draw a line on the pavement with chalk.
- Take turns with a friend to run up and jump when you reach the line.
- Mark where you land and measure each jump.

ON YOUR BIKE

Do you like whizzing along on a set of wheels? Check out these different tracks and bikes to pick the perfect pedal power for you.

TRACK CYCLING

Track cyclists reach high speeds on special lightweight bikes. They don't have brakes and only one gear. The riders crouch low to help them slip through the air easily.

Race on: smooth indoor track called a velodrome

Don't forget your: stretchy skin-suit

Best for: speed

ROAD RIDING

Road racers ride long distances in all weather. They carry water and energy food with them. Steep mountain roads and sprint finishes push their bodies to the limit.

Race on: flat roads and mountain climbs

Don't forget your: sunglasses

Best for: great views

Can you match these three helmets with the right kind of cycling?

1 Protects the face from flying stones.

2 Air holes keep the head cool.

3 Smooth shape for extra speed.

BMX RACING

BMX riders speed along specially built courses with sharp turns, dips and humps. They fly into the air and land with a bump as they race for the finish.

Race on: dirt tracks with bumps and jumps

Don't forget your: grippy gloves

Best for: cool tricks

MOUNTAIN BIKING

Mountain bikers race over rough country trails. They judder over rocks and whizz down stony slopes. Padded clothes protect them from falls.

Race on: steep hills and rocky tracks

Don't forget your: knee and elbow pads

Best for: thrills

IN THE POOL

Hit the pool for a watery workout. You need to learn speedy strokes, quick turns and high dives.

ACTIVITY

There are four swimming strokes to master. Can you spot them all in the pool?

- front crawl
- back stroke
- breast stroke
- butterfly

Crouch down on your starting block, then launch forward for a perfect racing dive

Do a quick "tumble turn" at the end of each length by rolling forward and pushing off the wall.

1

2

3

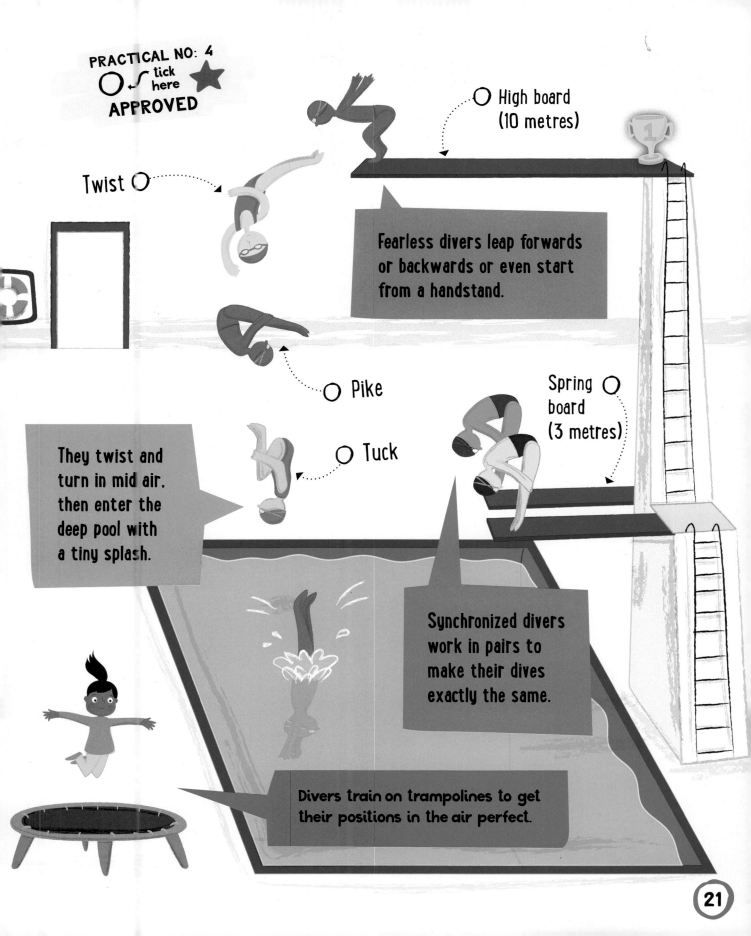

High board
(10 metres)

Twist ○

Fearless divers leap forwards or backwards or even start from a handstand.

○ Pike

Spring ○ board (3 metres)

○ Tuck

They twist and turn in mid air, then enter the deep pool with a tiny splash.

Synchronized divers work in pairs to make their dives exactly the same.

Divers train on trampolines to get their positions in the air perfect.

21

AGAINST THE CLOCK

It's race time and top athletes are going for gold! Every second counts, so technology is used to work out who has won

ON YOUR MARKS!

Bang! Swimmers, runners and cyclists burst into action as soon as they hear the electronic start pistol. The second it goes off, the clock automatically starts ticking...

BANG!

FALSE STARTS

The high-tech starting blocks sense movement if an athlete starts too soon.

FINISHES

At the track, the clock stops when the winner crosses a laser beam shining across the finish line.

Special tags on running shoes record each competitor's time as they cross the line.

The tag sends a signal to the reader.

···· the winner

1ST	01 : 49 : 63	WR
2ND	01 : 49 : 69	
3RD	01 : 50 : 03	

PHOTO FINISH

A high-speed camera takes a photo of the finish. This shows the winner in a close race.

▲ minutes   ▲ seconds   ▲ 10ths of a second

DEAD HEAT

When two athletes cross the line at exactly the same time, it is called a "dead heat".

CLOSE TIMES

Sometimes races can be so close that there are just fractions of a second between the first and third place.

BLINK OF AN EYE

A blink lasts for about three-tenths of a second.

SPORTING CHALLENGE

Letters after a finish time stand for:

WR – World Record
OR – Olympic Record
PB – Personal Best

Time yourself running the same distance three times. Your best time is your PB. Now try to beat it!

GYMNASTICS

Take your seat in the arena for a breathtaking display of different kinds of gymnastics.

ARTISTIC

Gymnasts need to be stretchy, strong and very brave. They swing from bars and rings, balance on a beam and spring over a vault.

pommel horse ·······

TRAINING TIP

Gymnasts dip their hands and feet in chalk dust to help them get a good grip.

There are squishy mats for safe landings.

ACROBATIC

Gymnasts work in pairs and teams to do dramatic balances to music.

beam

parallel bars

high bar

rings

vault

RHYTHMIC

Gymnasts throw, catch and balance objects as they dance gracefully across the floor. They compete in teams or on their own.

ribbon

hoop

rope

ball

FLOOR

Tricky tumbles, leaps, rolls and turns are performed to music on a large, springy mat.

Can you spot the five differences between the two pictures?

AMERICAN FOOTBALL

Your team has to get the ball to your opponent's end zone at the end of the field to score. Pass or run with the ball, quick!

PRACTICAL 5

BALL SPORTS

PRACTICAL NO: 5
tick here
APPROVED

BASKETBALL

Bounce and move with the ball, then throw it to a teammate. He shoots the ball into the basket. Two points!

Dribble the ball past these defenders, then boot it past the goalkeeper into the net... GOAL!

FOOTBALL

KIT BAG

This kit is worn to keep players safe.

- gloves
- face guard
- headgear

Find them in the pictures.

Join the Academy teams for some ball sports. The coaches are ready to help you get the hang of passing, throwing, dribbling, catching and kicking.

RUGBY

Catch! Now players will try to tackle you to the ground! Kick the ball over the bar to score, or grab it and run with it over the line!

27

BASEBALL

The kit:

The field:

bases

The players:
2 teams
9 players in each team.

fielder   batter   pitcher

The aim:
Teams take turns batting and fielding.
Batters hit the ball and score runs by
racing around all the bases and back
to the start. Fielders get batters out
with fast pitching and clever catching.

BATS AND RACKETS

Swot up on some smashing ball sports with these speedy facts.
Learn about fast balls, hard bats and springy rackets.

CRICKET

The kit:

The pitch:

boundary

The players:
2 teams
11 players in each team

stumps

bowler   batter   fielder

The aim:
Teams take turns batting and bowling.
Batters hit the ball and score by running
between two sets of stumps. The
fielding team get them out with a catch
or by hitting the stumps with the ball.

TENNIS

The court:

The kit:

The players:
2 players = singles
4 players = doubles

The aim:
Players stand on either side of the net and hit the ball back and forth. The ball can only bounce once before it is hit. If it goes outside the lines of the court or into the net, the other player gets a point.

Match up the balls and rackets.

ACTIVITY

Which sport uses this bat?
- ◯ squash
- ⊘ table tennis
- ◯ lacrosse

BADMINTON

The kit:

shuttlecock

The court:

The aim:
Players hit a light shuttlecock back and forth over a high net. If it lands in your court or you hit it into the net, the other player wins a point.

The players:
2 players = singles
4 players = doubles

THEORY NO: 7
◯ tick here
APPROVED

IN THE SNOW

You need to be fit and fearless to slide down snowy mountains at top speed. Hop on a chairlift and see what sports you can spot on the slopes down below.

VROOOM!
Top downhill skiers can travel at 153 kilometres per hour – that's faster than a speeding car!

When snowboarding first began it was called "snurfing" – snow + surfing.

TRAINING TIP

In the summer, when the snow melts, skiers and snowboarders keep fit with sports like surfing, cycling and skateboarding.

ACTIVITY

What is buried in the snow? Match each item with the correct word.

a)

b)

c)

d)

○ ski

○ ski pole

○ goggles

○ snowboard

THEORY NO: 8

○ ✓ tick here
APPROVED

CAN YOU FIND?

 ○ Slalom skiers zig-zagging between poles as they zoom downhill

 ○ Ski jumper leaning forwards as they launch off a steep ramp

 ○ Snowboarders doing tricks on rails and curved courses

 ○ Downhill skiers hurtling down steep slopes

ON THE ICE

Get your skates on for some slippery action on the ice!
Can you glide gracefully, speed smoothly
or zip about the rink with a stick?

FIGURE SKATING

Pull off some dramatic jumps, turns and dizzying spins in time to music. You will need to be very fit!

SPEED SKATING

Put on a sleek suit, then race around the rink. Special slippy gloves let your fingertips glide over the ice as you lean into the corners. Can you get the fastest lap time?

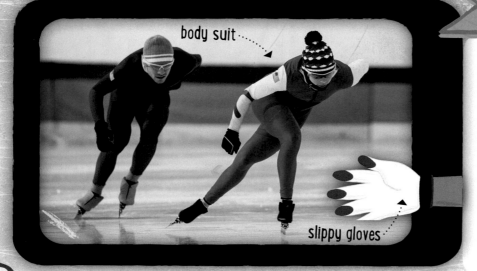

body suit

slippy gloves

ICE HOCKEY

Wear a helmet and plenty of padding for this tough game. Two teams of six players tear around the rink, pushing the "puck" from player to player with their sticks. Flip it past the goalie to score!

puck ·······▶

helmet ◀·····

padding

TRAINING TIP

Get super-quick with your hockey stick by practising off the ice. Move a small ball instead of a puck around a smooth surface.

ICE DANCING

No jumps, throws, or big lifts are allowed here. Just graceful dancing with a partner.

ACTIVITY

Can you pick the right skates for each sport?

1
A hard shoe and a long, narrow blade for going fast in one direction.

2
An elegant boot with a slim blade. Sharp toe spikes help with stops and spins.

3
A sturdy boot and a short, thick blade for quick changes of direction.

ON THE WATER

Find your way through the watery maze on the training lake, then try out some water sports with sails, paddles and oars.

PRACTICAL NO: 7

◯ ✓ tick here

APPROVED

START HERE

It takes skill to steer a yacht around the floating markers.

floating markers ┈┈┈►

◄┈┈┈ face this way

move this way ┈┈┈►

Pull on the oars to glide forwards in a rowing boat.

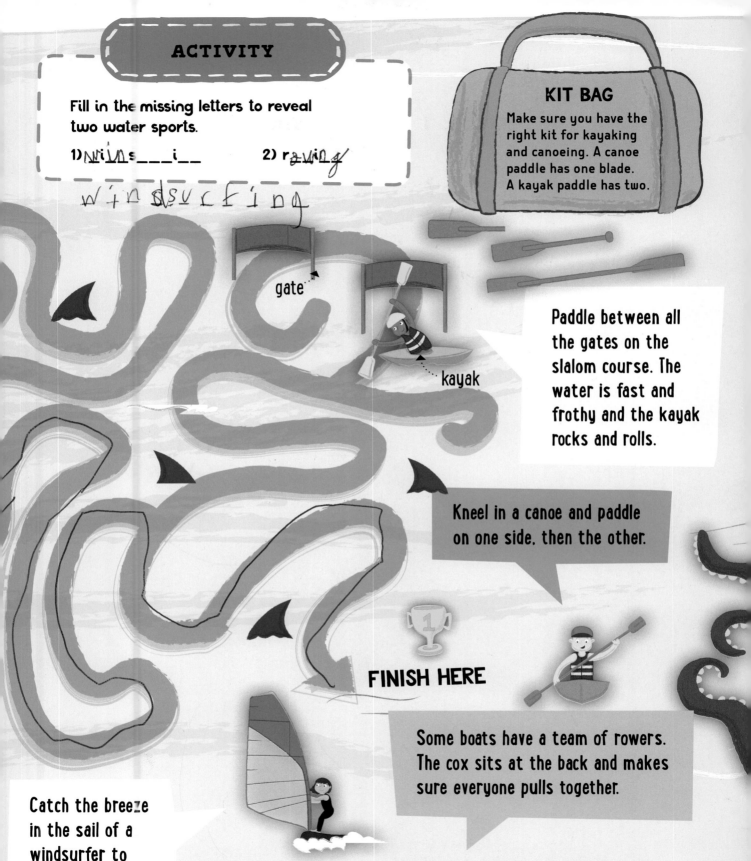

ACTIVITY

Fill in the missing letters to reveal two water sports.

1) W_nds___i__   2) r_ _ing

(handwritten: windsurfing, raving)

KIT BAG

Make sure you have the right kit for kayaking and canoeing. A canoe paddle has one blade. A kayak paddle has two.

gate

kayak

Paddle between all the gates on the slalom course. The water is fast and frothy and the kayak rocks and rolls.

Kneel in a canoe and paddle on one side, then the other.

FINISH HERE

Some boats have a team of rowers. The cox sits at the back and makes sure everyone pulls together.

Catch the breeze in the sail of a windsurfer to speed along.

cox

35

MARTIAL ARTS

Everywhere you look fighters are doing flying kicks. But don't worry, nobody gets hurt in martial arts training. Put on a suit and learn some fighting moves.

STRIKE!

BELT COLOURS

Belt colour hierarchy is different for different sports but generally white is for beginners and black is top level.

Find clues in the fact files to help you spot all the martial arts in the gym.

KICK!

Beginner fighters wear a white belt.

The most skilled fighters wear a black belt.

KARATE

AIM: Land well-aimed blows on your opponent with **strikes** from your hands or feet.

WEAR: A white suit called a gi

TAEKWONDO

AIM: Use different types of **kick** aimed at the face, body and neck.

WEAR: A white suit called a dobok

KIT: Head gear and body protection

THROW!

BLOCK!

TRAINING TIP

Practise your kicks and blows on squishy punch bags.

HOLD!

AIKIDO

AIM: **Block** your opponent, throw them, or trap them in a hold.

WEAR: Wide trousers called hakama

KIT: Wooden training weapons

JUDO

AIM: **Throw** your opponent to the ground or trap them in a **hold**.

WEAR: A suit called a judogi

37

COMPETITION TIME

Keep training hard and you could join a team of top athletes from your country to compete at the Olympics!

Can you give each athlete their correct medal?
gold
silver
bronze

THEORY NO: 9
tick here
APPROVED

3

1

2

TRAINING TIP

Most top athletes have trained for 10,000 hours by the time they win Olympic gold!

ALL SORTS OF SPORTS

There are many events at the Olympics. Can you match the pictures to the words?

- archery
- artistic swimming
- beach volleyball
- fencing
- show jumping
- trampolining
- water polo
- weight-lifting

a)
b)
c)
d)

e)
f)
g)
h)

TOP 5 OLYMPIC FACTS

1 The first Olympic Games took place in Ancient Greece about 3000 years ago.

2 The games are held every four years.

3 A different country hosts the Olympics each time.

4 There is a Winter Olympics and a Summer Olympics.

5 Teams from over 200 different countries compete in the Summer Olympics.

PARALYMPIC GAMES

Disabled athletes compete against each other in the Paralympics.

RECOVERY TIME

Smart watch

Congratulations, you made it through athlete training! Follow these steps for rest and recovery to get your body ready for your next big challenge.

COOL DOWN

Creak!

1 Gentle exercise helps your body to slow down after a workout.

EAT AND DRINK

Yum!

2 Refuel after exercise with water and a healthy snack.

RUB YOUR MUSCLES

Ouch!

3 Top athletes have a massage to ease aches and pains.

CHILL

Brrrr!

4 Ice packs and ice baths help sore muscles recover!

TAKE A BREAK

Hum!

5 Relax! Even the best athletes need a day off training.

SLEEP

Zzzzz!

6 Your body repairs itself when you are sleeping.

Sports stars do everything they can to keep their bodies in great shape.

DEEP SLEEP

Athletes sleep for up to ten hours a night. Many take naps after training too! Special smart watches show them how much restful sleep they are getting.

Can you find four differences between the two pictures?

DEEP BREATHS

This looks like a submarine, but it is actually an oxygen pod. Injured athletes climb inside and breathe in pure oxygen – that's a gas in the air. It helps them heal more quickly.

DEEP FREEZE

Athletes strip off and stand in a special chilly chamber for a few minutes. The air inside is cooled to –150ºC! This helps their bodies to recover after tough events.

BABE RUTH

Thought to be the greatest baseball player of all time. He played from 1914 to 1935 and hit 714 home runs in his career.

MICHAEL JORDAN

Jordan made the sport of basketbal popular throughout the world. He is one of the highest- scoring players of all time

USAIN BOLT

The lightning-fast Jamaican sprinter is the world's fastest man. In 2009 he broke the 100 metre world record, running it in 9.58 seconds.

LAURA KENNY

This British athlete is the most successful female track cyclist in Olympic history, and has won four Olympic gold medals

HALL OF FAME

TRISCHA ZORN

The most successful paralympic athlete ever. Being born blind did not stop her winning a total of 55 medals in swimming.

NADIA COMANECI

The first ever gymnast to score a perfect 10 at the Olympics! She won five Olympic gold medals altogether in her career.

MICHAEL PHELPS

Phelps won 18 Olympic medals in his career – more than any other athlete ever. His incredibly long arms helped make him a super-speedy swimmer.

PELÉ

Pelé won the World Cup with Brazil a record three times. He also holds the world record for the most goals scored in football – 1,283 goals!

These amazing athletes all made it to the top of their sport. Could you be next?

EXAMINATION

Now it's time to see how much you have learned.

1 Which foods are full of protein?
   a) Meat, fish and eggs
   b) Rice, pasta and potatoes
   c) Carrots, broccoli and apples

2 Which body part makes your pulse?
   a) Your lungs
   b) Your heart
   c) Your legs

3 Which of these is FALSE?
   a) O.R. stands for Old Record
   b) O.R. stands for Olympic Record

4 What do you do with a discus?
   a) Play it
   b) Dance to it
   c) Throw it

5 Which of these is TRUE?
   a) BMX riders race on dirt tracks.
   b) BMX riders race in a velodrome.

6 What do track runners have on their shoes?
   a) Spikes
   b) Lights
   c) Brakes

7 What is it called when two athletes finish a race at the same time?
   a) A head meet
   b) A dead neat
   c) A dead heat

8 Which of these is a type of dive?
   a) A pike
   b) A pipe
   c) A pool

9 Which of these objects does a rhythmic gymnast use?
   a) A hat
   b) A hoop
   c) A horn

10 In which sport is the ball thrown by a pitcher?
   a) Baseball
   b) Basketball
   c) Cricket

11 Which one of these is an Olympic sport?
   a) fencing
   b) hedging
   c) fetching

12 What is the name of the disk used in ice hockey?
   a) A pluck
   b) A chuck
   c) A puck

13 What do kayakers use to move forward?
   a) Oars
   b) Paddles
   c) Pedals

14 In which sport is it okay to kick other athletes?
   a) Archery
   b) Fencing
   c) Karate

15 What does sweat do?
   a) Warms you up
   b) Wears you out
   c) Cools you down

SPORTY SCORES

Check your answers at the back of the book and add up your score.

1 to 5 Oops! Get back to training and give your brain a workout.

6 to 10 Score! You are well on your way to becoming a winning athlete.

11 to 15 Record breaker! You could be the next sporting superstar!

SPORTS SPEAK

cox
The person in a rowing boat who instructs the rowers.

defender
A player whose job it is to stop the other team from scoring.

dribble
To kick, bounce or tap the ball quickly to keep it moving.

fencing
A sport where athletes fight each other using thin swords.

fielder
A player whose job is to try to catch the ball, while the batting team tries to hit the ball.

hurdle
A barrier that runners, called hurdlers, leap over in a race.

lacrosse
A game in which players use sticks with a net at the end to catch and throw a ball.

laser beam
A narrow beam of light produced by a machine.

opponent
The person who is playing against you in a sport.

slalom
A race on skis or in kayaks where the athletes follow a route which twists in and out between poles.

sprint
To run, ride or swim as fast as you can for a short distance.

squash
A racket game in which two players hit a small ball against the walls of the court.

synchronized
When athletes make the same move at the same time and speed as each other.

tackle
To take the ball off another player in football, or to knock a player to the ground in rugby.

SPORTS ACADEMY

WELL DONE!

You made it through your athlete's training.

Name

SPORTS STAR

FULLY QUALIFIED

ANSWERS

Page 6
Banana, trainers, water and stop watch

Page 7
A = road cyclist
B = wheelchair racer
C = baseball player
D = diver
E = pole vaulter

Page 15
Swimmer is wearing a sock, goggles on wrong way round, seal doesn't belong, no water in pool, swimmer is facing the wrong way

Page 17

Page 19
1 = mountain biking
2 = road racing
3 = track cycling

Page 20

Page 25

Pages 26-27

Page 29

The racket is for table tennis

Page 31

a = snowboard
b = goggles
c = ski pole
d = ski

Page 33
1 = speed skating
2 = figure skating and ice dancing
3 = ice hockey

Pages 34-35
Windsurfing and rowing

Page 36-37

Page 38
1 = Gold
2 = Silver
3 = Bronze

a = artistic swimming
b = show jumping
c = weight-lifting
d = trampolining
e = fencing
f = water polo
g = beach volleybal
h = archery

Page 41

Page 44-45
1 = a; 2 = b; 3 = a; 4 = c; 5 = a
6 = a; 7 = c; 8 = a; 9 = b; 10 = a;
11 = a; 12 = c; 13 = b; 14 = c; 15 = c.